The Water Is Wide

By David Neufeld

Celebration Press
Pearson Learning Group

Contents

1620

Billy Coppin's Story

My name is Billy Coppin and I love the sea. Maybe I would have spent most of my life in the British Navy if my parents hadn't taken me to America. They said we could live and worship the way we want to here.

I remember the day I stood on the deck of the *Mayflower* as it left the port of Plymouth, England. It was Wednesday, September 6, 1620. I was nine years old.

Passengers from the leaky ship *Speedwell* also climbed on board with us. The decks were crowded. All the passengers were nervous and happy at the same time. The captain hollered, "Cast off!" and we were on our way! We cleared the mouth of the harbor and the whole Atlantic lay before us.

The quarters below deck were crowded.
At night everyone lay down side by side
on the floor.

When I complained to John Howland,
another passenger, he teased, "I'll show
you tight quarters." Then he lifted me over
an empty barrel and said he'd add my
friends Wrestling Brewster and Gyles
Hopkins, too. After that I didn't complain.

Sometimes I slept up on deck under
a pile of canvas to keep warm. It was
wonderful watching the sails billowing
against the starry sky.

John Howland knew all about ships.
He showed Gyles, Wrestling, and me
how to tie sailor knots like the bowline.
He had us practice until we could tie
them with our eyes closed.

That was a useful skill to have on
the sea voyage. About our second
week out, the *Mayflower* met a fierce
storm. Thirty-foot seas washed over the
decks. The winds shrieked. Below the
decks everybody prayed in the dark. In
the middle of it all came a splintering
crash.

John hurried up on deck, and I followed
him up the ladder. Most of the crew was in
the rigging trying to save the sails. One of
the wooden spars used to help support a
sail was broken and lay on the deck tangled
in ropes. The wind and water were pushing
it toward the side of the ship. We had to
tie it down, or it would be lost.

"Put a bowline on that post," John yelled
as he tossed me a rope. Fighting the wind,
I struggled to tie the knot. John crossed
the slanted deck and wrapped the other
end of the rope around the spar.

The foaming sea broke over the side
of the ship and almost overturned us. I
grabbed the closest rail and held on as
tightly as I could, but the water lifted John
off his feet and carried him into the black
night. Then I saw his arms thrashing.
Luckily he was able to get hold of the rope
and clung tightly to it. He was hauled up
on deck, bruised and cut but alive.

After about two months at sea, I think I was probably the first person on the *Mayflower* to see land. I was on deck getting a bit of fresh air.

The cold wind reminded us that it could be well into November before we reached land. Still, most of us didn't expect the wind to be so bone chilling.

The sun, just up, struck our backs but didn't warm us. The captain was steering the ship. The sky behind us was clear, but there were dark clouds just above the horizon in the west. The sailor who had been in the crow's nest, near the top of the ship's mast, was standing on the deck talking with the captain.

I was looking at the bank of low, dark clouds, my face chapped from the brisk northerly wind. Then I noticed the waves breaking. I'd seen plenty of waves break at sea when two swells slapped together. Those waves don't linger, but these did! They kept foaming along the same line.

Now there's nothing more foolish than a fellow who's been at sea for two months crying "Land" when it's not there. So I started climbing up the ratlines, or rope ladder, toward the masthead to make sure I was right about what I saw.

Then all of a sudden I was sure I was really looking at land. I carefully climbed another rung higher. Just as the captain bellowed, "Off there, you," I said, "Land!" Then I yelled it loudly, "LAND!!!"

The sailor who had been talking to the captain climbed back up to the crow's nest in a hurry. "LAND HO!" he shouted.

The passengers began crowding onto the deck. "Are you certain?" they asked.

"Aye!" the sailor answered.

A shout of joy arose from the passengers and crew as we stared at a land that would be our new home. We expected to see hills and cliffs, but this new land was flat. Still, we were all thankful to have arrived safely in America.

That first winter was terrible. We were cold and hungry, and some were very sick. Everyone still lived on the *Mayflower.*

Just before the first snow, we laid out the main street through our new little village. Then we built three houses with thatched roofs, but the first one caught fire. Another one did too a month later.

By March many people were sick. Luckily, I was one of only seven people who weren't. My wonderful parents died, and so did about half the group, which deeply saddened me. Fortunately, a kind man named Tom Fuller adopted me soon after I lost my parents.

We were determined to build our new Plymouth to be like an English village. After all, we wanted this new land to feel like home. There was plenty of good timber around, so the men cut trees and shaped frames for houses. We children were set to making thatch from dried grasses for the roofs.

One day just as spring was beginning to show on the trees, a native walked down the street of the village. He said, "Welcome, Englishmen," just as clearly as could be. We learned that his name was Samoset.

The next week he brought an English-speaking Patuxet named Squanto. This man had been to Spain and England! When he was about nine, Squanto had been kidnapped by a crewman on an English ship. He was taken to Spain, where he was sold into slavery.

Some Spanish monks helped Squanto escape to England, where he lived for several years and learned to speak English. An English sea captain helped him get back home. When he returned to America, he found that his whole tribe had died from a strange sickness. He was the last living Patuxet.

Squanto was the interpreter for the chief of the Wampanoag tribe, Massasoit, when the chief wanted to talk to us. This chief showed us where to plant our crops. We

also signed a treaty with the Wampanoag, agreeing to help and protect each other.

On April 5, 1621, the *Mayflower* sailed for England. I stayed in America with Tom Fuller and others of our group. Soon I became a good sailor. I went with John Howland to fish in the small, open shallop from the *Mayflower.* Squanto showed us the best places for fishing, and we set up racks on the beach to dry the plentiful cod.

It was my job to tend one of Tom Fuller's fields that year, too. I grew corn and peas with the help of Elizabeth Brewster. She was only six years old, but she told me that she wanted to marry me when she grew up. I told her to be sure and get all the pods from the pea vines.

In autumn, after the harvest, we had a thanksgiving festival. It lasted three days. About 90 Indians came and brought more food. We ate outdoors at long tables and played games.

All too soon cold weather arrived again.
This time, though, we had well-thatched
houses and piles of firewood. We'd also
dried many pounds of cod to help us
through the winter, and the men hunted
almost every day for deer, moose, and bear.
Squanto said that we had enough, but an
early snow scared the elders. They didn't
say so, but I could see it in their faces.

The snow scared me, too. It made the
village look tiny. When the wind blew, snow
curled over the fences and settled on the
thatched roofs like clouds.

Another ship from England arrived the next spring. Tom helped me write this letter, which I sent to my grandfather when that ship returned.

April 1622

Dear Grandfather Coppin,

I am well. Tom Fuller is taking good care of me. I miss you, and of course I miss Mother and Father dreadfully. But now Tom has become like family and America seems like home.

It is spring here and wildflowers are everywhere Governor William Bradford thinks that we Plymouth children have to learn our letters, so Tom is teaching me to read and write.

A gale blew through here this past week. We had one awful night. Francis Cooke lost the thatch off his cottage roof and then stayed with William Bradford. The tall wooden fence around the village helped protect the animals from the worst of the storm.

I listened to the wind. It whined and whistled. It was like the storm we had when the Mayflower crossed the ocean. I was not afraid this time. That other storm ended, so I figured this one would, too. After two days the sun was shining again. We went out and got the scattered chickens.

We have lasted more than a full year in this land. The elders say we will be here hundreds of years. I believe they are right.

Your Grandson,
Billy

The O'Farrells Come to America

Adrian O'Farrell lived in County Cork, Ireland, with his father, his brother Michael, and his sister-in-law Fiona. Life in Ireland in 1846 was extremely hard. Adrian missed his brother Patrick, his sister-in-law Kate, and his cousin Edward. He longed to join them in America one day.

County Cork, Ireland
October 10, 1846

Dear Patrick,

How is America? I miss you and Kate and Edward and hope you are well. Father is well.

The potato crop failed. Each week we have had to sell some of Grandmother's silver to buy food.

Michael and Fiona are preparing to join you in New York. Father says I am too young to go.

Your brother,
Adrian

THE COUNTY CORK GAZETTE

County Cork, Ireland   January 27, 1847

FEVER KILLS RAPIDLY!

We regret to say that due to the spreading hunger, fever is increasing rapidly and becoming more deadly each day. Since our last issue, we have heard of many cases among our fellow citizens. This terrible disease has killed too many.

Sadly, Fiona's dream of seeing America was never fulfilled. She died of fever on January 19, 1847. Michael was grief-stricken, as was the rest of the family. When she was fighting for her life, Fiona begged Michael to go on to America without her. He refused, but after she died, he made arrangements to be in New York by late February.

18

County Cork, Ireland
February 10, 1847

Patrick, my son,

I've just been down to Cove. A ship from Liverpool, bound for New York, came into the port for repairs. On board were a large number of people in poor condition. They were almost totally without food or warm clothing.

I shudder to think what Michael may be enduring on his journey. Please write us the moment he arrives!

Your Loving Father

New York, New York
March 3, 1847

Dear Father and Adrian,

Michael has arrived and is with me and Kate. He speaks little of the voyage. There was a job waiting for him alongside me on the docks. There are so many Irishmen working with us that it is hard to believe we're not at home in County Cork. I hope that the work will take Michael's mind off his loss of Fiona.

Little Cousin Edward has grown four inches just this year. He will be tall like you, Father. Edward talks about Adrian all the time and hopes that one day soon you and he can join us here. It hurts not to have enough money for passage for you and Adrian right now.

Patrick

Over the next several months, more and more people suffered from hunger in Ireland because of the failure of the potato crop. The only food on some farms was boiled seaweed, which added to the spread of stomach problems. Adrian and his father may not have survived if Patrick had not scraped up a small amount of money to send them to buy food.

Robert Geary, a good friend of the O'Farrells, left Ireland for England, hoping to earn enough money to get to America. Adrian hoped Robert would soon get to see Patrick in New York. He wished he and Father could go, too.

The spirit of the holiday season strengthened Adrian's and his father's longing to be with their family in America. Adrian wanted his family to know he was thinking about them on Christmas Day.

County Cork, Ireland
December 25, 1847

Dear Patrick,

Happy holidays to you, Kate, Michael, and Edward. Father and I made a kidney pudding to take to our old friends the Gearys. They have had word from Robert. He has a job keeping accounts for a woolen mill in London.

We are doing our best to celebrate. The town is quiet. Mostly, Father and I are remembering holidays past when we were all together.

Your brother,
Adrian

Several months later, Patrick happened upon an old friend from home. John Fitzpatrick had made his way to America about ten years earlier and since then had done well.

Mr. Fitzpatrick began working as a common sailor, but now he owned a shipping company. His five ships traveled between New York and Panama.

He asked Patrick and Michael to work for him. He told them that his luck in America would rub off on them. Patrick believed that his family's luck might be changing. He couldn't wait to write to his father and Adrian to tell them the good news.

New York, New York
June 15, 1848

Dear Father and Adrian,

Do you remember Mr. Fitzpatrick, Father? We happened upon him a month ago. He remembered you. He wants us to open an office for his shipping company in the port of San Francisco. We are to find a building and hire workers. He has provided us with papers and funds.

We will sail to Panama, travel across land to the Pacific, and sail again from there to San Francisco. Mr. Fitzpatrick has given Edward a spyglass and assigned him the task of keeping watch for sea serpents! I have not seen Michael so interested in anything since he arrived. Perhaps he will be happy in California. Please be patient, as it may be months before we can write again.

Patrick

San Francisco, California
September 5, 1848

Dear Father and Adrian,

San Francisco is a lot like Ireland, as there are green hills, cliffs, and cool breezes off the ocean. Kate is delighted. Edward is in school! Michael looks heartier than I've ever seen him. We have rented a warehouse and will now set to work building a pier for Mr. Fitzpatrick's ships. He sent one of his ships around "the Horn," the tip of South America, so we can expect it within four months.

25

The voyage from New York to Panama was quite an adventure. We traveled through tropical waters. The weather was hotter than we've ever known.

We crossed the Isthmus of Panama, a narrow strip of land between the Atlantic and Pacific, on mules. In the company were many passengers bound for California. Some of them settled in San Francisco, so we have a few friends here already.

Patrick

Several months before the O'Farrells arrived, gold had been discovered in California. By the time they moved in, San Francisco had almost become a ghost town. Anyone with a pan or a pick and a shovel was leaving for the gold fields, and many were returning rich. Michael caught "gold fever" as well and wanted to try his luck.

He gathered what simple tools he could and left for the gold fields. Michael staked a claim on government-owned land along a river and began to pan for gold. He washed sand and gravel in his pan to separate out any pieces of gold.

Some months later a man rushed into the shipping office where Patrick worked with a letter from Michael. It said, "Patrick and Kate, I've found the end of a rainbow! Come quickly and bring a sturdy wagon."

In the area where Michael was searching, gold was located at or near the earth's surface. The riverbank was lined with sluices—long wood troughs in which sand and gravel were washed with water. The gold was caught in grooves. Sand and gravel were being washed and panned by the ton.

Patrick, Kate, and Edward took a wagon and met Michael at his claim. Afterward they arranged for Mr. Fitzpatrick's ships to carry Michael's and other prospectors' gold to New York.

As soon as he could, Patrick wrote his father and Adrian a letter.

San Francisco, California
May 2, 1849

Dear Father and Adrian,

We are rich! Michael has been successful in prospecting for gold where he staked a claim on public land! He is making more than enough to share with our family. In addition, Mr. Fitzpatrick says if we stick with him, we will want for nothing.

Enclosed is a draft for $1,000. Please join us. We need your good head for numbers, Father.

Edward has built a lookout on the pier. He spends many afternoons watching for incoming ships with his spyglass. It is very useful, as he gives us advance notice of ships that we are expecting.

Come quickly. Only a few more months and we shall all be together again!

Love,
Patrick

San Francisco Sun

JUNE 10, 1849

WHOLE TOWN EMPTIED AS INHABITANTS RUSH TO THE GOLD WASHINGS

Every seaport as far south as San Diego, every town, and nearly every farm near rivers and fields in which the gold has been found is drained of human beings.

THE COUNTY CORK GAZETTE

County Cork, Ireland

September 17, 1849

LOCAL MAN STRIKES IT RICH IN CALIFORNIA GOLD!

Michael O'Farrell, who joined his brother Patrick in America some months back, has washed thousands of dollars in gold out of the dirt of California in just five months. Now that's what we'd call taking in the wash!

Patrick was saddened in September by a letter from Robert Geary's parents. It said Patrick's father was too ill now to travel but wanted Adrian to go ahead. Robert was arranging Adrian's passage to America. His father hoped to recover soon and join the family

San Francisco, California   March 18, 1850

CALIFORNIA MONITOR

Notice: The sailing ship <u>Golden Eagle</u> arrived today with 71 passengers from the East Coast in 94 days, a record. Aboard the ship were Sean O'Farrell and Adrian O'Farrell, father and brother of Patrick O'Farrell, Agent of the East-West Shipping Company.

Patrick soon sent a letter to Robert Geary in County Cork.

> San Francisco, California
> March 30, 1850
>
> Dear Robert,
>
> We are all together now in California. Thank you for coming from London to County Cork to arrange passage for Father and Adrian. We are so glad that father braved the journey!
>
> He is a little weak, but he seems to be faring very well in the California climate. Adrian, too, is doing well. He and Edward are having a delightful time together.
>
> This is a good land. We have so much to share. The shipping company is growing fast, and we could use your help. Will you join us?
>
> Your friend,
> Patrick

1985

Lan Learns to Speak English

Tucson, Arizona
September 1, 1985

Dear Grandmother,

I miss you. I start school tomorrow. Tin says that they have special teachers to help us learn English. I hope so. When the children next door speak, they sound like chickens to me.

Your loving granddaughter,
Lan

Lan imagined her grandmother reading the letter and admiring its neat Vietnamese characters, for Lan had beautiful handwriting. Inside the letter were photos of Mama, Tin, Cadao, and herself in Tucson. Grandmother would be glad to see almond trees just like the ones in Vietnam.

* * * * * * * * * * *

"Welcome to Chitwood Elementary School," said a young man. He waited while a half dozen translators spoke to groups of immigrant children. Then the man, Mr. O'Hara, surprised Lan by saying hello and welcoming them first in Vietnamese, then in Cambodian, then in two other languages! "English is not an easy language, but it's the one spoken here. I hope by the end of the year you will like speaking it. Please call me Mr. O."

Some students laughed. Whenever she heard English now, Lan thought of chickens. Maybe other students had made comparisons, too.

Lan began to notice that Mr. O spoke only about objects that he had in front of him. He did things to the objects—threw the ball, cut the paper, broke the stick. He did this all morning until Lan's head buzzed.

Mr. O led the students to the cafeteria for lunch. The cafeteria was noisy, but Lan couldn't understand a word. She noticed other Asian students speaking English. How did they do that? How long had it taken them to learn this strange language?

"How was school, Lan?" her mother asked when she got home.

Lan was glad to hear her own language spoken. Most of the day, while she was in school, her mind had felt the way her body had on the boat when they escaped from Vietnam—tired and off balance. "I have a man teacher," Lan said.

"Is he nice?" her mother asked.

"He can speak our language, but he doesn't usually. Mostly he talks to the class in English," Lan said.

"Is he Vietnamese?" her mother asked.

"No, American. He throws balls and breaks sticks," Lan said.

"That sounds American," her mother laughed, "like baseball. I hope you are going to learn to speak English easily."

The next morning Mr. O's table was covered with more objects. There were fruits, articles of clothing, pieces of colored paper, school supplies, and toys.

"Come pick something," Mr. O said in English to a Cambodian girl. She walked to the front of the room and picked up a shoe.

"Shoe," said Mr. O. He made a motion for the girl to repeat the word. She said the word perfectly. Then Mr. O drew a picture of a foot on the board and said, "Foot. You wear a shoe on your foot."

Lan imagined herself saying "shoe" and "foot." Easy, she thought.

A boy walked up next and chose a purple piece of paper. Mr. O grinned. "Purple paper," he said.

The class burst out laughing at the funny sounds. The boy blushed.

"Everybody," Mr. O motioned. "Purple paper. Purple paper."

Lan didn't say anything. Her mother had learned a little English when the American soldiers were in Saigon, but that was before Lan was born. Her mother spoke only enough English to get them to America. She still believed that saying too much could get her in trouble because after the war, Vietnamese who had been friends to Americans were treated badly. Lan kept telling her mother they were safe now.

Mr. O motioned for Lan to come to the front of the class. Lan was eager to learn English, but she was nervous that she would embarrass herself in front of the other students.

Lan stood in front of the table. She knew all the fruits, so she chose a toy train. Their apartment was near a railroad track. Every evening at eight and every morning at five a train rumbled past, shaking the whole house.

"Train," Mr. O said. Lan looked at his mouth and made a *t* sound. Then Mr. O chose a toy truck from the table. "Truck," he said. "Trains and trucks carry people." Lan tried to repeat what he had said, but her tongue seemed to be tied in knots. "That was a good try, Lan," he said.

Then the weekend came, and Lan walked with her mother to the market. They bought rice noodles, dried shrimp, and some cans of pickled radishes and bean paste.

Lan passed children jumping rope, singing, and counting. English singing sounded quite nice.

When they returned, her brother Tin was watching TV. All the shows were in either English or Spanish. Tin was older, so he'd learned some English before they left Vietnam. Lan wasn't sure why Tin was laughing. Was it because he knew what the people on TV were saying or because they were doing such strange things?

Lan watched the screen. She wondered if the government officials told the people on TV what to say. They did in Vietnam, but here it seemed as if you could say almost anything.

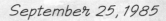

September 25, 1985

Dear Grandmother,

I am in school now. I have two friends who came here from Vietnam, but they're not from our city. I am learning English. They also teach us math. That is easier because it's only numbers.

Cadao is in school, too. He is learning English faster than I am. He can also speak some Spanish. Our neighbor from Mexico taught him. Cadao always was a chatterbox. I miss you.

Your loving granddaughter,
Lan

Mr. O had said it would happen. Several weeks later, on a Monday, American students joined the class. At first Mr. O had the students draw pictures—of their family, favorite fruit, or favorite animal. Afterward he explained, "Each of you will have a partner. Tell your partner about your drawing." Mr. O had two boxes. He had the students pick slips of paper from a box.

Lan picked number eight, her lucky number. An American girl with the same number came forward. "Lan, this is Becky."

"Hi! Nice to meet you," Becky said quickly. Lan was still trying to figure out what Becky had said when Becky started to describe the family members in her drawing.

Next it was Lan's turn to tell who was in her drawing. When she said her brother Cadao's name, Becky interrupted her.

Becky said, "I know your younger brother." Then she saw the confusion on Lan's face and slowed down a bit. Becky

pointed to her brother Leo's picture and to Cadao's picture and said, "They're friends."

Lan had understood some of the words. "Yes," she replied in English, "Leo and Cadao play."

"Do you have a friend here?" Becky asked.

A stream of Vietnamese spilled out of Lan's mouth. She blushed and started again, this time in English. "Yes, two from home—Vietnam."

"They came with you?" Becky asked.

"On other boat, other time," Lan said.

"In social studies we learned about people who left Vietnam in boats," Becky said. "They escaped to the United States." Lan could only understand "boats" and "Vietnam."

"Yes. I come in boat," Lan said.

Becky corrected Lan's sentence, "You came in a boat."

Lan quickly corrected herself, "Yes. I came in a boat."

"I'm afraid of boats," Becky said. "They tip." Lan watched Becky lean over in her chair.

Lan knew that Becky couldn't imagine what it was like. Becky probably hadn't been in the rain for days at a time. Becky probably hadn't been in an open boat in a storm at night.

"Yes. Not good," Lan said. "I like the land better."

Becky nodded in agreement.

One day, after more than two months of school had passed, Mr. O said, "I am proud of how much all of you are learning. To celebrate, we are going on a field trip today."

"The Arizona-Sonora Desert Museum is one of my favorite places in Tucson," he told them. Lan smiled. She understood everything he said.

The bus parked near a group of low adobe buildings. Boulders and ramps led to the museum's entrance. A guide welcomed them and said, "We have animals and plants from many parts of the desert."

Lan looked through a glass window at a rattlesnake. It reminded her of the different snakes in Vietnam. Then the class came to a screened-in area.

Its entrance had a special curtain that let people in but kept the birds from flying out. Before they went inside, Mr. O explained that small birds would fly close to them and that it was safe. The birds only wanted the nectar from the flowers he would give them to hold.

Next Mr. O gave a flower to each student. Lan put hers in her hair. Then he said, "Let's go inside and sit quietly on these benches."

Lan's class was very good at sitting quietly. After a few minutes a hummingbird came toward Lan. It hovered around her hair.

Lan remained very still. The little green bird hung in the air before her eyes. One red-throated bird landed on Mr. O's finger.

Lan closed her eyes and imagined she was back in Vietnam. Her grandmother, sitting beside her beneath an ancient tree, told Lan stories. The tree had lived through the war. There were still many hummingbirds. Lan began to feel that some things were beautiful in America, her new home, too.

Back in the classroom the next day, Mr. O said, "Thanksgiving vacation begins tomorrow." Then he explained the holiday's importance to Americans and showed pictures of the ship on which Pilgrims had sailed to their new homeland.

The ship reminded Lan of the U.S. Navy ship that picked up her family from a small boat near the Philippines. She raised her hand and said, "We came here on a boat, too."

Mr. O nodded his head. "Very good, Lan," he said, and asked if anyone else had come here on a boat. Several hands were raised. Mr. O told them they were like the Pilgrims and that this holiday is important for new people as well as for those who have been in America for a long time.

After school, Becky walked home with Lan and said, "My family would like your family to celebrate Thanksgiving with us tomorrow."

Lan smiled. She had understood every word. "I would like that," she said. "I'll check with my family first, but I'm sure they'll say yes." Thanksgiving wasn't just an American holiday to Lan now. It was her holiday, too!